To

Julie & Andy

From

Love Mom & Dad   Johnny & "Jo"
XOXO ' XOXO   XO XO ' XO XO

Merry Christmas !.

Dec. 2013

Published in Nashville, Tennessee, by Thomas Nelson. Thomas Nelson is a registered trademark of Thomas Nelson, Inc.

Compiled by Lisa Guest.

Cover and interior design by Thinkpen Design, Inc. www.thinkpendesign.com

Thomas Nelson, Inc., titles may be purchased in bulk for educational, business, fund-raising, or sales promotional use. For information, please e-mail SpecialMarkets@ThomasNelson.com.

Scripture quotations are taken from *The New King James Version*. © 1982, 1992 by Thomas Nelson, Inc. Used by permission. All rights reserved.

Grateful acknowledgment is made to all quoted authors and to the following publishers and copyright holders: Henry and Richard Blackaby, taken from *Discovering God's Daily Agenda*. Nashville, TN: Thomas Nelson, Inc., © 2007. Dietrich Bonhoeffer, taken from *A Testament to Freedom*. New York: HarperCollins. John Eldredge, taken from *Ransomed Heart* (blog), 18 December 2008 and 20 December 2009. Billy Graham, taken from *Billy Graham: The Inspirational Writings*. Nashville, TN: Thomas Nelson, Inc., © 2004. David Jeremiah, taken from *The Twelve Ways of Christmas*. Nashville, TN: Thomas Nelson, Inc., © 2008 David Jeremiah. Max Lucado, taken from *In the Grip of Grace*. Nashville, TN: Thomas Nelson, Inc., © 1996 Max Lucado. John MacArthur, taken from *The Miracle of Christmas*. Henri Nouwen, taken from *Gracias: A Latin American Journal*. Ronald Reagan, taken from *Dutch: A Memoir of Ronald Reagan* by Edmund Morris. New York: Random House, Inc. Charles R. Swindoll, taken from *The Finishing Touch*. Nashville, TN: Thomas Nelson, Inc., © 1994 Charles Swindoll. Philip Yancey, taken from *Finding God in Unexpected Places*. New York: Random House, Inc. Sarah Young, taken from *Jesus Calling*. Nashville, TN: Thomas Nelson, Inc., © 2004 Sarah Young.

ISBN: 978-1-4003-1840-7

Printed in China.

11 12 13 14 15 LEO 5 4 3 2 1

www.thomasnelson.com

Christmas

On This Holy Night

THOMAS NELSON
Since 1798

NASHVILLE   DALLAS   MEXICO CITY   RIO DE JANEIRO

Christmas — one night among millions, but it was enough to make us believe in miracles.

There is no way our little minds can comprehend the love of God. But that didn't keep Him from coming.

MAX LUCADO

Christmas offers its
wonderful message.
Immanuel.
God with us. . . .

He breathed our air, felt our pain,
knew our sorrows, and died for our sins.
He didn't come to frighten us,
but to show us the way to warmth and safety.

CHARLES R. SWINDOLL

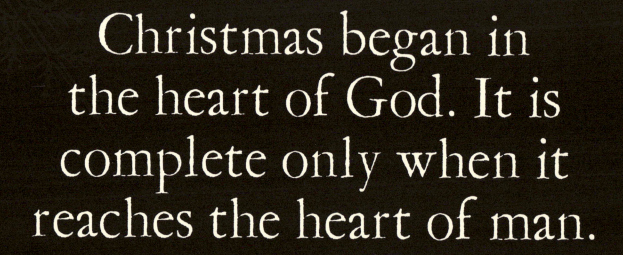

Christmas began in
the heart of God. It is
complete only when it
reaches the heart of man.

ANONYMOUS

Try to imagine what I gave up when
I came into your world as a baby.
I set aside My Glory, so that
I could identify with mankind. . . .
I became poor so that you might become rich.

SARAH YOUNG

This is Christmas. . . . God loving, searching, giving Himself – to us. Man's needing, receiving, giving himself – to God.

RUTH BELL GRAHAM

While the innkeeper tended to his guests, the devoted husband tended to his wife, and the shepherds tended to their flocks, a Child came to tend to their souls. And ours.

When Christ entered
our world, He didn't
come to brighten our
Decembers, but to
transform our lives.

RICH MILLER

The very purpose of Christ's coming into the world was that He might offer up His life as a sacrifice for the sins of men. He came to die. This is the heart of Christmas.

BILLY GRAHAM

Christmas is the
most stunning rescue
story of all time. . . .

Under cover of night, in a remote village in Palestine, in a world held captive by the dark prince, God comes to earth as a human being, a little boy. He invades the human race in order to rescue the human race.

JOHN ELDREDGE

Christmas is reassurance that God keeps His promises, then and now.

A prison cell, in which one waits, hopes . . .
and is completely dependent on the fact that
the door of freedom has to be opened from the
outside, is not a bad picture of Advent.

DIETRICH BONHOEFFER

Oh holy night . . . the Light entered the darkness, and everything changed.

One night . . . among the wrinkled hills of
Bethlehem . . . God, who knows no before or
after, entered time and space. God, who knows
no boundaries, took on the shocking confines of a
baby's skin, the ominous restraints of mortality.

PHILIP YANCEY

Think of the originality that went into the first Christmas. . . . No one but the Creator Himself would have scripted it that way.

DAVID JEREMIAH

She didn't expect to be pregnant. He didn't expect an angel to tell him to marry her anyway. The shepherds didn't expect the night shift to be anything unusual. God enters our lives in the most unexpected ways, but always with a perfect plan.

Christmas – the idea
of divine love was
wrapped up in a Person.

HALFORD E. LUCCOCK

For God so loved the world that He gave His
only begotten Son, that whoever believes in Him
should not perish but have everlasting life.

JOHN 3:16

God walked down the
stairs of heaven with a
Baby in His arms.

PAUL SCHERER

Mary didn't know whether
to give Him milk or give Him praise,
but she gave Him both since He was,
as near as she could figure, hungry and holy.

MAX LUCADO

God became man.
Marvel at the mystery.

Joseph didn't know whether to call Him
Junior or Father. But in the end called Him Jesus,
since that's what the angel said and since
he didn't have the faintest idea what to name
a God he could cradle in his arms.

MAX LUCADO

Christmas allows us to redefine "impossible."

The angel answered and said to her,
"The Holy Spirit will come upon you, and the
power of the Highest will overshadow you;
therefore, also, that Holy One who is to
be born will be called the Son of God. . . .
For with God nothing will be impossible."

LUKE 1:35, 37

The Lord Himself will give you a sign: Behold, the virgin shall conceive and bear a Son, and shall call His name Immanuel.

ISAIAH 7:14

The greatest gift God gives is His presence.
His name is Immanuel–God with us.

HENRY AND RICHARD BLACKABY

Christmas is to forget ourselves in the service of others.

HENRY C. LINK

It is Christmas every time you let God love others through you. . . . Yes, it is Christmas every time you smile at your brother and offer him your hand.

MOTHER TERESA

The newborn Child
was comforted in the
arms of His mother.
For eternity His people
will be comforted
by the strong arm
of His Father.

And she brought forth her firstborn Son,
and wrapped Him in swaddling cloths,
and laid Him in a manger, because there
was no room for them in the inn.

LUKE 2:7

On that first Christmas,
Truth incarnate didn't need
the world's press. . . .

No newspapers covered the story. No CNN®. No Internet. Yet God's history-changing entrance into the world is still well remembered and celebrated centuries later.

On that sleepy, star-spangled night, those angels peeled back the sky just like you would tear open a sparkling Christmas present. . . .

Then with light and joy pouring out of
heaven like water through a broken dam,
they began to shout and sing the message
that baby Jesus had been born. . . .
The angels called it "good news," and it was.

LARRY LIBBY

Sometimes . . . we forget the true meaning of Christmas— the birth of the Prince of Peace, Jesus Christ.

RONALD REAGAN

For unto us a Child is born, Unto us a Son is given; And the government will be upon His shoulder. And His name will be called Wonderful, Counselor, Mighty God, Everlasting Father, Prince of Peace.

ISAIAH 9:6

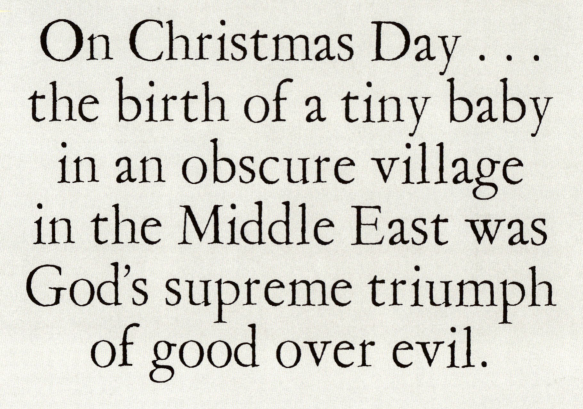

On Christmas Day . . .
the birth of a tiny baby
in an obscure village
in the Middle East was
God's supreme triumph
of good over evil.

CHARLES COLSON

Our freedom has come in an unexpected way.
Freedom from the consequences of sin, gained for us
by One born of peasants in a truck-stop town in Judea.

The way to Christmas lies through . . . a little gate, child-high, child-wide, and there is a password: "Peace on earth to men of good will."

ANGELO PATRI

And suddenly there was with the angel a
multitude of the heavenly host praising God
and saying: "Glory to God in the highest,
And on earth peace, goodwill toward men!"

LUKE 2:13-14

On that holy night,
God sent *His* Son to save
our sons and daughters.

Jesus came *from* heaven to offer us a way
to heaven. This is the Christmas story.

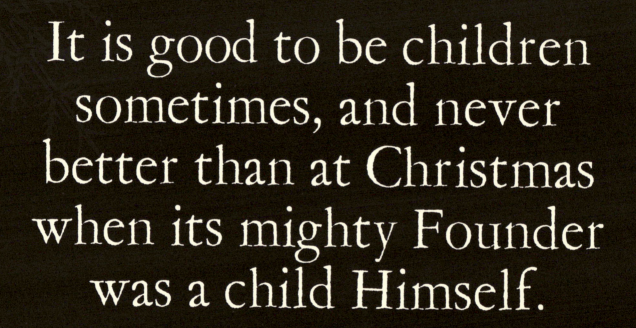

It is good to be children sometimes, and never better than at Christmas when its mighty Founder was a child Himself.

CHARLES DICKENS

And this will be the sign to you: You will find a
Babe wrapped in swaddling cloths, lying in a manger.

LUKE 2:12

If we only focus on the birth of Jesus as a sweet story, . . . then we miss out on what can happen for us tonight. . . .

The God who comes to be with us
can take the shabby, hurting, dirty,
abandoned, humiliating parts of ourselves
and will make them and us new.

JENNIE C. OLBRYCH

Christmas. . . .
We cannot prepare for
an observance. We must
prepare for an experience.

HANDEL H. BROWN

Then the angel said to them, "Do not be afraid, for behold, I bring you good tidings of great joy which will be to all people. For there is born to you this day in the city of David a Savior, who is Christ the Lord."

LUKE 2:10-11

God saw what the world
most desperately needed,
and what He chose to give
us was Himself. . . . This is
the message of Christmas.

JOHN ELDREDGE

The Son of God became a man
to enable men to become the sons of God.

C. S. LEWIS

If we could condense all the truths of Christmas into only three words, these would be the words: "God with us." . . .

More astonishing than a baby in the manger is the
truth that this promised baby is the omnipotent
Creator of the heavens and the earth!

JOHN MACARTHUR

On Christmas, heavenly glories were exchanged for a humble humanity.

If Christ had been born to a princess mother and a knighted father, in a well-appointed nursery behind castle walls, would we easily believe that He wanted to be our friend, much less our Savior?

Wise men still seek Him.

ANONYMOUS

After Jesus was born in Bethlehem of Judea, . . . wise men from the East came to Jerusalem, saying, "Where is He who has been born King of the Jews? For we have seen His star in the East and have come to worship Him."

MATTHEW 2:1-2

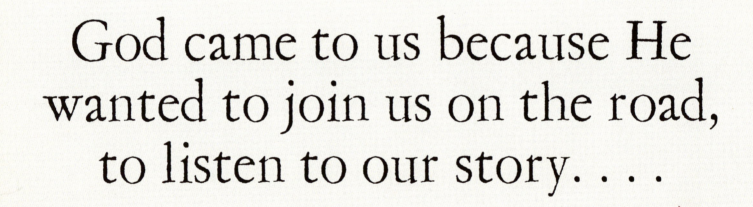

God came to us because He
wanted to join us on the road,
to listen to our story. . . .

This is the great mystery of Christmas that
continues to give us comfort and consolation:
we are not alone on our journey.

HENRI NOUWEN

A thrill of hope the weary world rejoices, . . . O night divine, the night when Christ was born.

PLACIDE CAPPEAU DE ROQUEMAURE,

TRANSLATED BY JOHN SULLIVAN DWIGHT